Eternal Security

Eternal Security

by
John MacArthur, Jr.

WORD OF GRACE COMMUNICATIONS
P.O. Box 4000
Panorama City, CA 91412

© 1989 by
JOHN F. MACARTHUR, JR.

All Scripture quotations, unless noted otherwise, are from the *New Scofield Reference Bible*, King James Version. Copyright © 1967 by Oxford University Press, Inc. Reprinted by permission.

Library of Congress Cataloging in Publication Data

MacArthur, John, 1939-
    Eternal security / by John MacArthur, Jr.
      p.   cm. — (John MacArthur's Bible studies)
    Includes indexes.
    ISBN 0-8024-5373-2
    1. Bible. N.T. Romans V, 1-11—Criticism, interpretation, etc.
2. Salvation—Biblical teaching. 3. Assurance (Theology)—Biblical
teaching. I. Title. II. Series: MacArthur, John, 1939-   Bible
studies.
BS2665.2.M187   1989
227'.106—dc19   88-37062
                                                  CIP

1 2 3 4 Printing/LC/Year 91 90 89

Printed in the United States of America

Contents

These Bible studies are taken from messages delivered by Pastor-Teacher John MacArthur, Jr., at Grace Community Church in Panorama City, California. These messages have been combined into a 4-tape album entitled *Eternal Security*. You may purchase this series either in an attractive vinyl cassette album or as individual cassettes. To purchase these tapes, request the album *Eternal Security*, or ask for the tapes by their individual GC numbers. Please consult the current price list; then, send your order, making your check payable to:

WORD OF GRACE COMMUNICATIONS
P.O. Box 4000
Panorama City, CA 91412

Or call the following toll-free number:
1-800-55-GRACE

1

The Security of Salvation—Part 1

Outline

Introduction
A. The Debate on Eternal Security
B. The Defense of Eternal Security
    1. The incomprehensibility of grace
    2. The insistence on works

Lesson
I. Peace with God (v. 1)
  A. A Righteous Relationship
  B. A Reconciled Relationship
    1. The nature of the war
     a) Its reality
     b) Its ramifications
       (1) Deuteronomy 32:21-22
       (2) Isaiah 13:9, 13
       (3) Nahum 1:2
       (4) Ephesians 5:6
       (5) Revelation 19:15
       (6) Psalm 7:11
    2. The nature of the peace
     a) Past propitiation through the cross
       (1) The satisfaction for sin
       (2) The sacrifice of Christ
     b) Present peace through cleansing
       (1) The truths of reconciliation
         (*a*) Eternal peace
         (*b*) Present peace
       (2) The time of reconciliation
       (3) The tranquillity of reconciliation

Introduction

A. The Debate on Eternal Security

Throughout the years, eternal security has been a hotly debated issue in theology. Many theologians say you can lose your salvation, and many claim you cannot. The doctrine of eternal security is sometimes referred to as "the perseverance of the saints" or "once saved, always saved." Today, however, many people believe a Christian can lose his salvation. Such a person is considered to have backslidden—to have fallen away from Christ.

The doctrine that claims a person can lose his salvation makes salvation conditional. It says that since God has saved us, we will maintain our salvation as we continue to match up with God's standard. But if we fail at any point we lose it. That is a works-righteousness perspective.

B. The Defense of Eternal Security

The apostle Paul addresses the issue of eternal security in Romans 5. Many treatments of this subject don't include Romans 5, yet it is arguably the most definitive text ever written on the security of our salvation.

Paul's purpose in the epistle of Romans is to affirm the gospel. In chapters 3-4 his thesis is that salvation comes by grace through faith.

1. The incomprehensibility of grace

That thesis was revolutionary to the Jewish people, who had been reared on a works-righteousness system of salvation. They believed that by doing certain works they would gain God's favor. Virtually all other world religions teach the same thing: that man must live up to some religious code or ethical standard to be saved. Unredeemed man finds it difficult to comprehend that salvation is a free gift of God's grace, unearned and undeserved, appropriated by faith alone.

2. The insistence on works

Paul had the Jewish people in mind when he wrote Romans 5—he had just completed a treatise on Abraham as an illustration of justification by faith in the previous section, Romans 3:21–4:25. A Jewish person would tend to doubt that faith is all that is needed for salvation. It would be difficult for him to believe that faith would be enough to save him from the condemnation of God on Judgment Day.

In Romans 5 Paul speaks directly to that issue. Today if you espouse the doctrine of eternal security, someone will invariably ask you, "You mean that after you become a Christian there's no standard? Doesn't your salvation depend on your obedience?" Paul addresses those questions in Romans 5:1-11. He presents six links in a chain that eternally ties a true believer to the Savior.

9

Lesson

I. PEACE WITH GOD (v. 1)

"Therefore, being justified by faith, we have peace with God through our Lord Jesus Christ."

A. A Righteous Relationship

The word *therefore* links verse 1 to the foundation Paul has laid in chapters 3-4. Justification by faith—being made right with God through faith in Christ—initially ushers us into salvation. When you believe in the Lord Jesus Christ you obtain salvation and an inheritance in eternity filled with blessing. One of those blessings is security: you have peace with God through our Lord Jesus Christ.

B. A Reconciled Relationship

What is the peace we have with God? Some have suggested we have tranquillity of mind—a psychological sense of security. But that is not the intention of the passage. It is not subjective peace; it is objective. It does not refer to feelings but to a relationship.

If we have peace with God because of salvation, what did we have prior to salvation? War—the opposite of peace. Christ changed our relationship to God dramatically. We were at war with God. He was our enemy, and we were His enemy. But through justification by faith in Christ, God brought us into a relationship of peace. That peace is not an attitude of psychological tranquillity or a calm mind. Peace with God means our war with Him is over.

1. The nature of the war

Most people think they've never been at war with God. But the Bible says that before you come to Christ you're at war with God (cf. Col. 1:21-22). Some non-Christians will claim to be religious—to believe in God and be concerned about what He thinks. They don't see themselves as enemies of God actively striking blows at God's kingdom.

a) Its reality

The issue is not that they are at war with God, but that God is at war with them. The majority of people don't see themselves as fighting God. But God is their enemy, whether they are consciously His enemy or not. In fact, the war is so severe that God will someday cast the unbeliever into an eternal lake of fire to burn for eternity. God is at war with the sinner because He is the enemy of sin and sin's father, Satan. If you're not a child of God, you're a child of Satan (John 1:12; 8:44).

The background of this concept is given in Romans 1-2, which describes the wrath of God. Romans 1:18 says, "The wrath of God is revealed from heaven against all ungodliness and unrighteousness of men, who hold the truth in unrighteousness." God is at war with the ungodly and the unrighteous—those who don't know Christ. First Corinthians 16:22 says, "If any man love not the Lord Jesus Christ, let him be Anathema [cursed]."

b) Its ramifications

(1) Deuteronomy 32:21-22—"They have moved me to jealousy with that which is not God; they have provoked me to anger with their vanities: and I will move them to jealousy with those who are not a people; I will provoke them to anger with a foolish nation. For a fire is kindled in mine anger, and shall burn unto the lowest hell, and shall consume the earth with her increase, and set on fire the foundations of the mountains." God is furious with sinners.

(2) Isaiah 13:9, 13—"The day of the Lord cometh, cruel both with wrath and fierce anger, to lay the land desolate; and he shall destroy the sinners out of it. . . . Therefore, I will shake the heavens, and the earth shall remove out of its place, in the wrath of the Lord of hosts, and in the day of his fierce anger."

(3) Nahum 1:2—"God is jealous, and the Lord avengeth; the Lord avengeth, and is furious; the Lord will take vengeance on his adversaries, and he reserveth wrath for his enemies."

(4) Ephesians 5:6—"Let no man deceive you with vain words; for because of these things cometh the wrath of God upon the sons of disobedience."

(5) Revelation 19:15—When Jesus returns, "out of his mouth goeth a sharp sword, that with it he should smite the nations, and he shall rule them with a rod of iron; and he treadeth the winepress of the fierceness and wrath of Almighty God."

(6) Psalm 7:11—"God judgeth the righteous, and God is angry with the wicked every day." That is the sum of God's attitude: He is at war with the wicked.

2. The nature of the peace

   a) Past propitiation through the cross

      (1) The satisfaction for sin

         We have peace with God, and we didn't do anything to obtain that peace. God poured out His vengeance, anger, and wrath on Christ, and God was appeased. Our new status is peace with God, and it was accomplished by Christ's reconciling work on the cross.

         Christ made full payment for our sins, and God was propitiated—a theological term meaning He was satisfied. Colossians 1:20-22 speaks of His "having made peace through the blood of his cross . . . . you, that were once alienated and enemies in your mind by wicked works, yet now hath he reconciled in the body of his flesh through death, to present you holy and unblamable and unreprovable in his sight." Jesus Christ

12

so fully accomplished peace with God that from now on, you are forever holy and faultless in His sight. Why? Because Christ bore every sin for which you and I should have been punished.

The Reality of Reconciliation

Justification and reconciliation are distinguishable as terms, but they are inseparable in reality. Justification embraces reconciliation (Rom. 5), sanctification (Rom. 6-7), and glorification (Rom. 8). When you embrace Jesus Christ by faith and are justified, inherent in that justification is the anticipation of glorification, the process of sanctification, and reconciliation to God (Rom. 8:30). We are no longer the enemy but sons, crying, "Abba, Father"—the Aramaic equivalent to "Daddy" (Gal. 4:6).

(2) The sacrifice of Christ

The wrath of God, which ultimately could have consigned us to eternal hell, is removed. All God's fury was fully absorbed in the sacrifice of Jesus Christ. We are left with the marvelous reconciliation accomplished "through our Lord Jesus Christ" (Rom. 5:1). Ephesians 1:3 says that God has "blessed us with all spiritual blessings in heavenly places in Christ." Everything is ours because of Christ. He not only reconciled us to God, but also gave us the ministry of reconciliation, which is to preach the gospel to those in need of reconciliation (2 Cor. 5:18-21).

b) Present peace through cleansing

How does God maintain His relationship with us? Jesus not only reconciled us to God, but also maintains that relationship. That is His high-priestly work. He keeps on cleansing us from all sin (1 John 1:7).

(1) The truths of reconciliation

(*a*) Eternal peace

We are forever at peace with God because every sin we will commit has already been paid for by Christ. Therefore nothing can destroy our relationship with Him.

(*b*) Present peace

Every day that we sin, the Lord keeps on cleansing us—maintaining our relationship with Him—through the past act of Christ on the cross and His present mediation at the right hand of God. In His high-priestly ministry "he ever liveth to make intercession for [us]" (Heb. 7:25).

(2) The time of reconciliation

How long does Christ make intercession? For as long as Jesus Christ lives—and He lives forever. When a person embraces Christ by faith, the spotless Son of God makes him one with God.

(3) The tranquillity of reconciliation

I believe that peace with God produces a sense of tranquillity within us. That's not the meaning of Romans 1, but peace with God certainly makes me feel good. Theologian Charles Hodge called it "that sweet quiet of the soul" (*Commentary on the Epistle to the Romans* [Grand Rapids: Eerdmans, 1974], p. 132). I'm a son of God and a brother of Jesus Christ. I'm in His family, and God is at peace with me.

Ephesians 2:14 says of Christ: "He is our peace." As long as He lives, which is forever, He will maintain our peace with God. God is satisfied with Christ's sacrifice for our sin, His wrath is gone, and we are at peace. Nothing can change that. In Hebrews 8:12 God says, "I will be merciful to their unrighteousness, and their sins and their iniquities will I remember no more."

14

II. STANDING IN GRACE (v. 2a)

"By whom [Christ] also we have access by faith into this grace in which we stand."

We are not moving in and out of grace; we are standing in grace.

A. The Mediation of Christ

The key to this passage is the mediation of Jesus Christ. Through His death He brings us to God.

1. Inaccessibility to God

Verse 2 says, "By whom also we have access by faith." The Greek word translated "access" was used two other times to speak of access to God (Eph. 2:18; 3:12). That would have been a shocking, incomprehensible concept for the Jewish people of Paul's day to comprehend, and to some extent it still is. They had been taught that God was holy and unapproachable. They knew from the past that if they ever came close to God they would be consumed.

a) The unapproachable One

Exodus 19:9-25 illustrates the Jewish concept of approaching God. As God prepared to give Israel the law from Mount Sinai, "the Lord said unto Moses, Lo, I come unto thee in a thick cloud, that the people may hear when I speak with thee, and believe thee forever. And Moses told the words of the people unto the Lord. And the Lord said unto Moses, Go unto the people, and sanctify them today and tomorrow, and let them wash their clothes, and be ready on the third day; for the third day the Lord will come down in the sight of all the people upon Mount Sinai. And thou shall set bounds unto the people round about, saying, Take heed to yourselves, that ye go not up into the mount, or touch the border of it. Whosoever toucheth the mount shall be surely put to death: there shall not an hand touch it, but he shall surely be stoned, or shot through; whether it be beast or man, it shall not live: when the trumpet soundeth long, they shall come up to the mount.

"And Moses went down from the mount unto the people, and sanctified the people; and they washed their clothes. And he said unto the people, Be ready on the third day: come not near your wives. And it shall come to pass on the third day in the morning, that there were thunders and lightnings, and a thick cloud upon the mount, and the voice of the trumpet exceedingly loud, so that all the people that were in the camp trembled. And Moses brought forth the people out of the camp to meet with God; and they stood at the lower part of the mount. And Mount Sinai was altogether in a smoke, because the Lord descended upon it in fire; and the smoke thereof ascended as the smoke of a furnace, and the whole mount quaked greatly. And when the voice of the trumpet sounded long, and became louder and louder, Moses spoke, and God answered him by a voice.

"And the Lord came down upon Mount Sinai, on the top of the mount; and the Lord called Moses up to the top of the mount, and Moses went up. And the Lord said unto Moses, Go down, charge the people, lest they break through unto the Lord to gaze, and many of them perish. And let the priests also, who come near to the Lord, sanctify themselves, lest the Lord break forth upon them. And Moses said unto the Lord, The people cannot come up to Mount Sinai; for thou chargedst us, saying, Set bounds about the mount, and sanctify it. And the Lord said unto him, Away, get thee down, and thou shalt come up, thou, and Aaron with thee; but let not the priests and the people break through to come up unto the Lord, lest He break forth upon them. So Moses went down unto the people, and spoke unto them."

b) The unholy people

After God led His people out of Egypt, He established that they had only limited access to Him. Why? Because He is holy, and man is utterly unholy.

(1) The limitations

Even after God established the Tabernacle and then the Temple, the people could come only so close. There were different limitations for Gentiles, for Jewish women, for Jewish men, and for priests. Only the high priest could enter into the presence of God, and then only one day a year. After going through rigorous cleansing rituals, he entered the Holy of Holies, sprinkled blood on the altar, and left as quickly as he could.

(2) The lesson

Those who tried to approach God apart from His procedure died on the spot. Nadab and Abihu "offered strange fire before the Lord" and died immediately (Lev. 10:1-2). Korah, Dathan, and Abiram challenged the leadership of Moses and Aaron and tried to function as priests. However, the ground swallowed them up (Num. 16:1-35).

The Jewish people knew God was unapproachable. Access was not a word in their religious vocabulary. Even today sinful man has no access to God.

2. Accessibility through Christ

Christ's death changed the Old Testament view of access to God. Matthew 27:51 says that the moment Christ died, the veil of the Temple was torn from top to bottom—a symbol that access to God was now possible.

a) Hebrews 4:16—"Let us, therefore, come boldly unto the throne of grace, that we may obtain mercy, and find grace to help in time of need."

b) Jeremiah 32:38, 40—These words reflect God's promised New Covenant with His people: "They shall be my people, and I will be their God . . . I will not turn away from doing them good, but I will put my fear in their hearts, that they shall not depart from Me."

c) Hebrews 10:19-22—"Having therefore, brethren, boldness to enter into the holiest by the blood of Jesus, by a new and living way, which he hath consecrated for us, through the veil, that is to say, his flesh, and having an high priest over the house of God, let us draw near."

A frequent secular use of the Greek word translated "access" is of a haven or harbor for a ship in distress. Similarly, God is both a haven and a harbor for us in our distress.

B. The Medium of Grace

When we enter into the presence of God, we stand in grace (Rom. 5:2). That's why Hebrews 4:16 tells us to come boldly before God to obtain mercy. The Greek word translated "stand" (*histēmi*) means to "stand firm" or "abide." We are abiding in a state of grace.

1. The definition of grace

Grace is God's unmerited favor by which He saves us and makes us righteous. It is based solely on His sovereign love, which is manifested in the perfect sacrifice of Jesus Christ for our sin. It is not the result of any worthiness on our part. Once we are saved we stand in grace.

2. The definitiveness of grace

Many people believe that once someone is saved by grace he has to keep himself saved by keeping the law. But Romans 5:2 says that once we are truly saved, we stand in grace—firmly fixed in an environment of grace.

a) Jude 24—"Unto him that is able to keep you from falling, and to present you faultless before the presence of his glory with exceeding joy." When you are saved you stand in grace. It is a continual reality because of the high-priestly work of Christ. You stand in an aura of grace—grace that is continually forgiving and able to keep you from falling.

b) John 15:7—Jesus said, "Abide in me." We abide in an environment of grace. We're secure in that environ-

18

ment. We didn't do anything to get in; we can't do anything to get out.

c) Romans 5:20—"The law entered, that the offense might abound. But where sin abounded, grace did much more abound." There is no way out. Grace functions where there is failure, so every time you sin, grace covers your failure. That's why you're so secure. If salvation depended on our ability to obey rules, we would all lose our salvation.

We have peace with God, and we stand in grace. If someone asserts that peace with God can't secure our salvation, he would have to deny two things: (1) that the sacrifice of Christ is adequate to cover all sin and keep the peace, and (2) that maintaining that peace is beyond the ability of Christ, who "ever liveth to make intercession for [us]" (Heb. 7:25). So he would be denying who Christ is and His past and present work.

Maintaining the Peace

The high-priestly work of Christ is continuing right now. He maintains our peace with God and applies His grace to us. Romans 5:10 says, "If, when we were enemies, we were reconciled to God by the death of his Son, much more, being reconciled, we shall be saved by his life." Since a dying Savior succeeded in bringing us to God, a living Savior can certainly keep us there.

It is Christ's high-priestly work to go continually before the Father on our behalf. In Luke 22:31-32 Jesus says, "Simon, Simon, behold, Satan hath desired to have you. . . . but I have prayed for thee." That example gives us insight into how Christ maintains our relationship to God. Christ intercedes on our behalf to maintain our peace with God and our environment of grace.

Will the Judge Change His Verdict?

Arthur Pink, who wrote a book on the topic of eternal security (*Eternal Security* [Grand Rapids: Baker, 1974]), said, "It is utterly and absolutely impossible that the sentence of the divine Judge should ever be revoked or reversed. . . . Sooner shall the lightnings of omnipotence shiver the Rock of Ages than those sheltering in Him again be brought under condemnation" (*The Doctrines of Election and Justification* [Grand Rapids: Baker, 1974], pp. 247-48). The Judge issued a verdict that will stand forever.

1. 2 Timothy 1:12—The apostle Paul, confident of God's ability to preserve his salvation, said, "[I] am persuaded that he is able to keep that which I have committed unto him against that day."

2. Hebrews 10:10-14—"We are sanctified through the offering of the body of Jesus Christ once for all. And every priest standeth daily ministering and offering often the same sacrifices, which can never take away sins; but this man [Christ], after he had offered one sacrifice for sins forever, sat down on the right hand of God, from henceforth expecting till his enemies be made his footstool. For by one offering he hath perfected forever them that are sanctified."

3. Romans 8:31-34—"If God be for us, who can be against us? He that spared not his own Son, but delivered him up for us all, how shall he not with him also freely give us all things?" (vv. 31-32). Since God gave the supreme gift of His Son to redeem us, you can be sure He will give us whatever is necessary to preserve our redemption.

   Verses 33-34 say, "Who shall lay any thing to the charge of God's elect? Shall God that justified? Who is he that condemneth? Shall Christ that died, yea rather, that is risen again, who is even at the right hand of God, who also maketh intercession for us?" Do you think the Attorney for our defense is going to accuse us? Do you think the Judge who delivered us from judgment and set us free is going to reverse His verdict? No!

Conclusion

Our peace with God and standing in grace are not precarious—we are on firm ground. God holds us, and that's His work. But it is our responsibility to obey Him. Why? Because one of the ways God keeps us is by empowering us with His Spirit to walk in obedience. When you see someone who once claimed to be a Christian but abandons the faith, remember 1 John 2:19: "They went out from us, but they were not of us; for if they had been of us, they would no doubt have continued with us." True Christians continue to persevere.

If anyone attacks the security of the believer, first of all he is attacking God and claiming that God changed His verdict. Second, he is attacking Christ and claiming that Christ's work on the cross was inadequate and that His high-priestly work can't maintain us. Finally, he is attacking the Holy Spirit and claiming that the Holy Spirit is inadequate to help the believer persevere. A discrediting of the Trinity is wrapped up in a denial of the security of salvation.

The nineteenth-century Scottish Presbyterian poet and preacher Horatius Bonar wrote these majestic words in a hymn entitled, "The Sin-Bearer" (*Hymns of Faith and Hope* [London: James Nisbett, 1872], pp. 100-102):

> Thy works, not mine, O Christ,
> > Speak gladness to this heart;
> They tell me all is done;
> > They bid my fear depart.
>
> To whom, save Thee,
> > Who can alone
> For sin atone,
> > Lord, shall I flee?
>
> Thy pains, not mine, O Christ,
> > Upon the shameful tree
> Have paid the law's full price,
> > And purchased peace for me.
>
> Thy tears, not mine, O Christ,
> > Have wept my guilt away;
> And turned this night of mine
> > Into a blessed day.
>
> Thy bonds, not mine, O Christ,
> > Unbind me of my chain,
> And break my prison-doors,
> > Ne'er to be barred again.

Thy wounds, not mine, O Christ,
　　Can heal my bruised soul;
Thy stripes, not mine, contain
　　The balm that makes me whole.

Thy blood, not mine, O Christ,
　　Thy blood so freely spilt,
Can blanch my blackest stains,
　　And purge away my guilt.

Thy cross, not mine, O Christ,
　　Has borne the awful load
Of sins, that none in heaven
　　Or earth could bear, but God.

Thy death, not mine, O Christ,
　　Has paid the ransom due;
Ten thousand deaths like mine,
　　Would have been all too few.

Thy righteousness, O Christ,
　　Alone can cover me;
No righteousness avails
　　Save that which is of Thee.

Thy righteousness alone
　　Can clothe and beautify;
I wrap it round my soul;
　　In this I'll live and die.

Focusing on the Facts

1. According to those who claim you can lose your salvation, what maintains salvation (see p. 8)?
2. Why did Paul write Romans (see p. 9)?
3. Why did the Jewish people have trouble understanding salvation by faith (see p. 9)?
4. When do we have peace with God (see p. 10)?
5. What kind of peace do we have (see p. 10)?
6. Explain the nature of unregenerate man's war with God (see pp. 10-11).

7. How do believers obtain peace with God (see p. 12)?
8. What happened to our sins (see pp. 12-13)?
9. How does Christ maintain our reconciliation to God (see pp. 13-14)?
10. How long does Christ maintain that reconciliation (see p. 14)?
11. How are we able to stand in grace (see p. 15)?
12. Why is "access" a key word in Romans 5:2 (see p. 15)?
13. What did the Jewish people in Old Testament times believe about approaching God? Why (see pp. 15-17)?
14. What enables man to have access to God (see p. 17)?
15. Define grace (see p. 18).
16. What did Paul mean when he said the believer stands in grace (Rom. 5:2; see p. 18)?
17. According to Romans 5:20, what must exist for grace to function (see p. 19)?
18. What is the significance of Romans 5:10 concerning our peace with God (see p. 19)?
19. How does a believer's obedience relate to his peace with God and standing in grace (see pp. 20-21)?

Pondering the Principles

1. Have you ever thought you could lose your salvation? Why? Read Romans 3:21–4:25 and 1 John 5:9-13. List as many reasons as you can find that show your salvation is real. How do they relate to the reasons you gave for losing your salvation? How does your peace with God relate to those truths? Thank God that you do not have to earn your salvation. Ask Him to make those truths fixed in your mind.

2. Read 2 Corinthians 5:17-21. According to Paul, all Christians have been given the ministry of reconciliation. What are some ways you personally can be involved as an ambassador for Christ? Based on the fact that you have peace with God, what has to be an integral part of your ministry? Make a list of people you know whom you'd like to see at peace with God. Begin praying that God would use you in bringing about their reconciliation with Him.

3. Since you now have access into God's presence and stand in grace, with what attitude should you approach God? Look up

the following verses: Hebrews 4:14-16; 10:12-22; 1 John 3:18-21; 4:17; 5:14. Why is it possible for us to have that attitude? List some reasons that explain why sometimes we don't approach God in that way. Read 1 John 1:9. Remember it is confession of sin that enables us to keep our consciences clean (Heb. 10:22) and be obedient to God. Although we can approach Him confidently, we must also approach Him with humility (James 4:10).

2
The Security of Salvation—Part 2

Outline

Introduction
A. Harmony and Righteousness
B. Humanity and Religion
C. Hope and Riches
   1. The guarantee of the Spirit
   2. The glory of the saints

Review
 I. Peace with God (v. 1)
II. Standing in Grace (v. 2*a*)

Lesson
III. Hope of Glory (vv. 2*b*-5*a*)
   A. The Praise of Our Hope (v. 2*b*)
      1. The gift of God
        a) Rejoicing in a secure future
        b) Hoping in a secure future
      2. The glory of God
        a) The redemption of glory
        b) The reflection of glory
        c) The recognition of glory
   B. The Proof of Our Hope (vv. 3-4)
      1. The purpose of tribulation
      2. The products of tribulation
        a) "Patience"
        b) "Experience"
          (1) The recognition
          (2) The reinforcement
          (3) The reward
          (4) The refinement

c) "Hope"

C. The Promise of Our Hope (v. 5*a*)

Introduction

The message of Romans 5:1-11 is simple: you can't lose your salvation. It is forever, eternal, everlasting, and unchanging. In 1 Peter 1:5 Peter says we "are kept by the power of God." Without question the most comforting, most assuring, and most joy-producing of all Christian truth is that our salvation is forever. The believer's joy and comfort depends on his assurance of his salvation. In Romans 5 Paul affirms that our salvation is secure in the power of God.

A. Harmony and Righteousness

Paul begins the epistle of Romans by discussing God's wrath against sinful men (1:1–3:20). Then he explains how to escape from that wrath in 3:21–4:25. If one wholeheartedly believes in the person and work of the Lord Jesus Christ, he is justified (made right with God). There is no work or self-effort involved—it is simply a matter of believing what God has done in Christ.

B. Humanity and Religion

That simple plan of salvation was difficult for the Jewish people to understand because they were reared in a works-oriented religious system. It also was difficult for Gentiles, who adhered to religions based on human achievement (a description of all false religion). To hear that all they need do was believe in the Lord Jesus Christ and they would be made right with God was more than they could have hoped for. Their natural inclination was to think that kind of salvation was too easy—that it wouldn't be enough to save them from condemnation on the Day of Judgment. Therefore Paul approaches Romans 5 in such a way to assure them of their salvation.

C. Hope and Riches

1. The guarantee of the Spirit

   Ephesians 1:13 says, "After ye believed, ye were sealed with the Holy Spirit of promise." That means you were stamped permanently as the possession of God. Ephesians 1:14 says the Holy Spirit is the "earnest" of your inheritance (Gk., *arrabōn*)—the down payment or guarantee of your salvation.

2. The glory of the saints

   After articulating the gospel of salvation, Paul said, "After I heard of your faith in the Lord Jesus, and love unto all the saints, [I] cease not to give thanks for you, making mention of you in my prayers: that the God of our Lord Jesus Christ, the Father of glory, may give unto you the spirit of wisdom and revelation in the knowledge of him, the eyes of your understanding being enlightened; that ye may know what is the hope of his calling, and what the riches of the glory of his inheritance in the saints" (Eph. 1:15-18). Paul wanted the Ephesian Christians to comprehend what they had been given in Christ. What Christ began in their lives He would ultimately fulfill.

Review

In Romans 5:1-11 Paul gives us six links in a chain that eternally secures us to the Savior. When the enemy hits you with doubt about the reality of your salvation, you can retreat to the promises of this passage.

I. PEACE WITH GOD (v. 1; see pp. 10-14)

"Therefore, being justified by faith, we have peace with God through our Lord Jesus Christ."

God is at war with men whether men are consciously at war with Him. But Christ bore the wrath of God on the cross and became our substitute, having received the punishment meant for us. As a result, those who trust in Him have peace with God. Isaiah 32:17 says, "The work of righteousness shall be peace; and the effect of righteousness, quietness and assurance forever."

II. STANDING IN GRACE (v. 2a; see pp. 15-20)

"By whom also we have access by faith into this grace in which we stand."

Is It Possible to Fall from Grace?

People who argue that a believer can fall from grace deny that salvation is secure. They base that conclusion on Galatians 5:4: "Christ is become of no effect unto you, whosoever of you are justified by the law; ye are fallen from grace." Paul did say it was possible to fall from grace, but notice to whom he said it. Paul was addressing people who tried to be saved by law. Verse 2 says, "Behold, I, Paul, say unto you, that if ye be circumcised, Christ shall profit you nothing." Christ can't do you any good if you believe you can be saved by some kind of physical operation. Then in verse 4 Paul says, "Christ is become of no effect unto you, whosoever of you are justified by the law." If you think you can be made right with God by keeping the law or by your own self-righteousness, Christ is useless to you.

Those kind of people have fallen from grace—from the grace principle of salvation. So Galatians 5:4 gives us commentary on the fate of those who attempt to come to God in some way other than through grace. A Christian standing in grace cannot fall out of grace. Galatians 5:5 says, "We through the Spirit wait for the hope of righteousness by faith"—not by law.

Lesson

III. HOPE OF GLORY (vv. 2b-5a)

We exult, or actually boast, "in hope of the glory of God" (Rom. 5:2). God has promised us future glory. Romans 8:28-29 says, "We know that all things work together for good to them that love God, to them who are the called according to his purpose. For whom he did foreknow, he also did predestinate to be conformed to the image of his Son." God didn't just predestine our initiation into salvation; He predestined the completion of it.

Romans 8:30 says, "Whom he did predestinate, them he also called; and whom he called, them he also justified; and whom he justified, them he also glorified." If you're predestined to begin, you're predestined to end. If you're predestined to be in Christ, you're predestined to be like Christ. The hope of the believer and the doctrine of security are based on the hope of glory.

Security—Past, Present, and Future

The first three links in the chain of security need to be drawn together. First, the security of the believer is anchored in the past—Christ made peace with God. Second, the security of the believer is anchored and maintained in the present—we stand in grace, and Christ lives to intercede on our behalf. And third, the security of the believer is anchored in the future—our future glory is guaranteed because we have been redeemed to exult in hope of ultimate glory. The past, present, and future work of God unite to secure the believer forever.

A. The Praise of Our Hope (v. 2*b*)

"[We] rejoice in hope of the glory of God."

1. The gift of God

a) Rejoicing in a secure future

The Greek word translated "rejoice" (*kauchaomai*) refers to a confident boast or exultant jubilation. It is a strong word that speaks of rejoicing at the highest level. We rejoice in a secure future. We have no fear because Christ said, "All that the Father giveth me shall come to me. . . . I should lose nothing, but should raise [them] up again at the last day" (John 6:37, 39).

b) Hoping in a secure future

First Timothy 1:1 says that our Savior, Jesus Christ, is our hope. First Peter 1:18-21 explains, "Forasmuch as ye know that ye were not redeemed with corruptible things, like silver and gold, from your vain manner of life received by tradition from your fathers, but with the precious blood of Christ, as of a lamb without blemish and without spot, who verily was foreordained before the foundation of the world, but was manifest in these last times for you, who by him do believe in God, who raised him up from the dead and gave him glory, that your faith and hope might be in God." Since God raised up Jesus from the grave, we can trust Him to raise us up by the same promise.

In John 17:22 Jesus prays, "The glory which thou gavest me I have given them." At that time the fulfillment of Christ's prayer was yet future. It still remains future for us, but we have the hope of ultimate glorification. Our rejoicing in future glory is not based on our own worthiness; it is based on the promise and power of God.

2. The glory of God

Romans 5:2 says, "[We] rejoice in hope of the glory of God." The glory of God is the expression of God's person—His intrinsic revelation of Himself. Someday God in the fullest and purest way will reflect His eternal character through us.

a) The redemption of glory

In Romans 8:18 Paul says, "I reckon that the sufferings of this present time are not worthy to be compared with the glory which shall be revealed in us." One day God will pour through us His eternal, infinite glory. Verse 19 says, "The earnest expectation of the creation waiteth for the manifestation of the sons of God." Right now "we have this treasure in earthen vessels" (2 Cor. 4:7). We are limited. But we and all creation are "waiting for the adoption, that is, the redemption of our body. For we are saved by hope" (Rom. 8:23-24).

What is our hope? We hope to lose our humanness—our earthiness—and become glorified, eternal persons through whom God can reveal His glory. The consummation of our redemption and the ultimate fulfillment of our salvation is the manifestation of God's glory in us.

The Flashing Crown of Jewels

There's no need for a lamp in heaven because the Lord is light (Rev. 21:23; 22:5). Much of heaven is transparent: the streets are made of sheer gold, and the layers and foundations are made of jewels through which the glory of God will radiate (Rev. 21:11-21). Heaven must be like an incomprehensible flashing crown of jewels as the glory of God radiates out of every refracted element. We will be caught up in that incredible display of glory and become eternal reflectors of the full majesty and glory of our infinite and majestic God.

However, it is impossible for us to glorify God in that way while we are in our present bodies. That's why we groan, waiting for the redemption of our bodies. Jesus will return in power and great glory (Matt. 24:30), and His blazing glory will be radiated through us.

b) The reflection of glory

(1) Romans 8:29—We will "be conformed to the image of his Son." We're going to be like Jesus. When He was transfigured before the disciples, He gave them but a glimpse of God's full glory, yet they were shaken to the core of their being (Matt. 17:1-8).

(2) 2 Corinthians 3:18—"We all, with unveiled face beholding as in a mirror the glory of the Lord, are changed into the same image from glory to glory." Even now, as we gaze on the glory of the Lord, we are being changed.

Moses is the illustration of the passage. In Exodus 34:29-35 God revealed His glory to Moses, and it caused his face to shine. The people were afraid of Him. So Moses veiled his face because he didn't want the people to see that the glory was fading (cf. 2 Cor. 3:13). In our human bodies the glory fades fast. The revelation of God's after-glow didn't last in Moses' case. But there will come a time when we will be lifted from one level of glory to another level of glory, until we reach that ultimate level of glory: when we become the image of Jesus Christ manifesting the full glory of God.

(3) Philippians 3:20-21—"Our citizenship is in heaven, from which also we look for the Savior, the Lord Jesus Christ, who shall change our lowly body, that it may be fashioned like his glorious body."

(4) Colossians 3:4—"When Christ, who is our life, shall appear, then shall ye also appear with him in glory."

(5) Hebrews 2:9-10—Jesus was "crowned with glory and honor, that he, by the grace of God, should taste death for every man. For it became him, for whom are all things, and by whom are all things, in bringing many sons unto glory." God's purpose in saving us was to bring us to glory. We were redeemed to be glorified. Christ is our salvation captain who brings many sons to glory through what He suffered (Heb. 2:10).

(6) Romans 9:23—"That he might make known the riches of his glory on the vessels of mercy, which he had before prepared unto glory." Those of us who are ordained to glory are ordained through mercy, not because we deserved it. Any other thought misconstrues the reality of our redemption.

(7) 1 Corinthians 2:7—"We speak the wisdom of God in a mystery, even the hidden wisdom, which God ordained before the ages unto our glory."

(8) 2 Corinthians 4:17—"Our light affliction, which is but for a moment, worketh for us a far more exceeding and eternal weight of glory."

(9) Colossians 1:27—"Christ in you [is] the hope of glory."

(10) 1 Thessalonians 2:12—"Walk worthy of God, who hath called you unto his kingdom and glory."

(11) 1 Peter 5:1—"The elders who are among you I exhort, who am also an elder, and a witness of the sufferings of Christ, and also a partaker of the glory that shall be revealed."

c) The recognition of glory

Does all that mean you can do what you want to do and still be glorified? Hebrews 3:6 says, "Christ [is] a Son over his own house, whose house are we, if we hold fast the confidence and the rejoicing of the hope firm unto the end." Our hope is secured by God. We prove we belong to God when we hold firm our confidence in that hope. Perseverance is a proof of salvation. Those who are truly part of the house of God will not depart from the faith. The one who wanders into sin and believes he'll be glorified no matter how he lives proves he never belonged to the household of God.

God not only secures His own but also implants within His own the power of the Spirit to keep alive their hope and obedience to the faith. God will keep His promise to those who are genuine. Hebrews 3:14 affirms that truth: "We are made partakers of Christ, if we hold the beginning of our confidence steadfast unto the end." That doesn't mean you remain saved by hanging on; it means you reveal you are saved by hanging on.

The Solid Rock of Hope

In "The Solid Rock" the nineteenth-century hymn writer Edward
Mote said:

> My hope is built on nothing less
>   Than Jesus' blood and righteousness;
> I dare not trust the sweetest frame
>   But wholly lean on Jesus' name.
>
> When darkness veils His lovely face,
>   I rest on His unchanging grace.
> In ev'ry high and stormy gale
>   My anchor holds within the veil.
>
> His oath, His covenant, His blood,
>   Support me in the whelming flood;
> When all around my soul gives way,
>   He then is all my hope and stay.
>
> On Christ, the solid rock, I stand,
>   All other ground is sinking sand,
>   All other ground is sinking sand.

B. The Proof of Our Hope (vv. 3-4)

"We glory [rejoice] in tribulations also, knowing that tribulation worketh patience; and patience, experience [charac-
ter]; and experience, hope."

1. The purpose of tribulation

The believer rejoices not only in the glory to come, but
also in present tribulation. Tribulation produces the
kind of character that has a greater capacity to rejoice
about the future. Why? Because no matter how severe
or devastating our trials are, they can never take away
our promised glory, steal our hope, or touch our joy. So
when we are faced with tribulation, we don't curse God
or question Him like the rest of the world, but rejoice in
the good that comes from it.

2. The products of tribulation

The Greek word translated "tribulation" (*thlipsis*) means "pressure." It was used in reference to squeezing olives for oil or squeezing grapes for wine. When the pressure is on, the oil and wine of rejoicing oozes out of us. The words that follow explain why.

a) "Patience"

Tribulation works patience (Gk., *hupomonē*, "patient endurance"). When you experience trouble, you learn to endure. The more troubles you have, the more you learn to endure.

b) "Experience"

Endurance produces "experience" (Gk., *dokimēn*). The verb form is *dokimazō*, which means, "to be approved" or "to put to the test for the purpose of approving." It has the same sense as testing gold or silver to remove the impurities.

(1) The recognition

A good way to translate *dokimēn* is "proven character." Since it is used of metal, it is similar to the way we use the word *sterling*, as in sterling silver. We also say someone has a sterling character when he has no observable flaws.

(2) The reinforcement

Through tribulation we learn to trust God. It is not a problem for us because it is an honor to suffer for Christ (1 Pet. 4:14). It also is a joy to learn to experience His sustaining power in the midst of suffering (Phil. 3:8-10). Tribulation increases our faith, purges us, sanctifies us, and strengthens us. It is like spiritual weight-lifting—it builds our spiritual muscles and raises our level of holiness.

(3) The reward

When we face tribulation we have reason to rejoice. We don't have to wait until we get to heaven to rejoice. That's because Scripture says our troubles build proven character.

James 1:12 says, "Blessed is the man that endureth temptation; for when he is tried, he shall receive the crown of life." The stronger we grow spiritually the richer our hope and the greater our rejoicing becomes. That's because the greater the reward awaiting us in heaven, the greater joy we will have in receiving it and in turn casting it before the feet of Jesus.

(4) The refinement

Salvation doesn't instantaneously refine character. If a bitter, angry, cantankerous person becomes saved, he is a bitter, angry, cantankerous Christian. However, salvation has planted within him the capacity to be perfected. After salvation the purging process begins—the Lord uses trials and tribulations to improve your character.

c) "Hope"

One thing trials can never do is take away your future hope, because that is secure. No matter how bad the attacks or how severe the tribulations, they do nothing but strengthen your spiritual character. That's why 1 Thessalonians 3:3 says, "No man should be moved by these afflictions; for ye yourselves know that we are appointed to these things."

C. The Promise of Our Hope (v. 5a)

"Hope maketh not ashamed."

Hope is never disappointed. You don't have to be ashamed of God. You will never come to the point where you say, "I put all my faith in Christ, and He deceived me." Hope will not be ashamed when it is in Jesus Christ.

Hope will never be disappointed, because it will receive the promised glory. We are at peace with God through Christ's death on the cross, we stand in grace, and we have a promised future glory. I am not ashamed to tell anyone that one day I will be in glory with Jesus Christ, radiating the eternal glory of God. That's my destiny. When you come to Jesus Christ and embrace Him, you will never be disappointed—your hope is secure.

Focusing on the Facts

1. According to Ephesians 1:13, what is the significance of the Holy Spirit in salvation (see p. 27)?
2. What was Paul's prayer for the Ephesians (Eph. 1:15-18; see p. 27)?
3. What kind of people fall from grace (see p. 28)?
4. What reason do Christians have for rejoicing (see p. 29)?
5. Rejoicing should be based on what (see p. 30)?
6. What is the "glory of God" that Paul refers to in Romans 5:2 (see p. 30)?
7. What is the Christian's hope (see p. 31)?
8. What was God's purpose in saving man (Heb. 2:9-10; see p. 32)?
9. How are believers ordained to glory (see p. 32)?
10. What is one way a person can prove he is a true believer (Heb. 3:6; see p. 33)?
11. How is the believer able to do that (see p. 33)?
12. Why is it important to rejoice in the midst of tribulation (see p. 34)?
13. What does tribulation do for our character? How (see pp. 35-36)?
14. Why will our hope not be disappointed (see pp. 36-37)?

Pondering the Principles

1. In Romans 8:29 Paul says that God had predestined us to be conformed to the image of His Son. What does that mean to you? Look up the following verses: Romans 13:14; 1 Corinthians 15:49; Ephesians 1:4; 4:24; Philippians 3:20-21; 1 John 3:2. Identify the verses that refer to our present obligations and those that

refer to our future glorification. What similarities can you find between our present and future? What contrasts? Does the goal of your life need to change? Ask God to confirm in your own heart the emphasis of your life.

2. According to Hebrews 3:6, 14, we are to hold fast our confidence of future glory to the end. Look up the following verses: Matthew 10:22; 24:13; Colossians 1:21-23; Hebrews 4:9-11; 6:10-11; 10:23. Why is it important for us to endure? How should you respond to that knowledge? Is your confidence in other things besides the hope of future glory? If so, what kind of effect have those things had on your security in your salvation? Put your confidence in God alone. Thank Him for His faithfulness in bringing you to glory.

3. How do you respond to tribulation? Why? What are some trials you are presently experiencing? According to Romans 5:3-4, how should you be responding to them? Ask God to give you the wisdom to respond in the appropriate manner.

3
The Security of Salvation—Part 3

Outline

Introduction
A. The Unfaithfulness of Man
B. The Faithfulness of God
    1. He keeps His promises
        a) Deuteronomy 7:9
        b) Isaiah 11:5
        c) Psalm 36:5
        d) Lamentations 3:23
        e) Hebrews 10:23
    2. He preserves His people
        a) 1 Thessalonians 5:23-24
        b) Philippians 1:6

Review
  I. Peace with God (v. 1)
 II. Standing in Grace (v. 2*a*)
III. Hope of Glory (vv. 2*b*-5*a*)

Lesson
IV. Possession of Love (vv. 5*b*-8)
    A. The Heart of Love (v. 5*b*)
        1. The internal reality
            a) Awareness
            b) Assurance
                (1) The presence of the Spirit
                (2) The absence of the Spirit
            c) Affection
        2. The internal river
        3. The internal revealer

Introduction

A. The Unfaithfulness of Man

We live in a day of unfaithfulness. Man cannot be trusted—he doesn't keep his promises. That's true of both individuals and nations. Husbands are often unfaithful to the vows they made to their wives. Wives are often unfaithful to their husbands. Children are often unfaithful to the principles taught by their parents. Parents are often unfaithful to meet the needs of their children. Employees are often unfaithful to the promises they make to their employers. And employers are often unfaithful to fulfill their obligations and responsibilities to their employees. We also have to acknowledge that Christians are often unfaithful to

God, although God is never unfaithful to them. Not one of us can claim immunity from the sin of unfaithfulness.

B. The Faithfulness of God

Only God is always faithful and keeps every promise in full. That fact is vital because everything we believe stands on the faithfulness of God. Our eternal destiny is at stake. In contrast to the unfaithfulness around us, it is refreshing to lift our eyes to our beloved God, who is always faithful.

1. He keeps His promises

Scripture is replete with verses that declare God's faithfulness.

a) Deuteronomy 7:9—"Know, therefore, that the Lord thy God, he is God, the faithful God."

b) Isaiah 11:5—"Faithfulness [is] the belt about [God's] waist" (NASB). Faithfulness encompasses God and holds all His other attributes in place.

c) Psalm 36:5—"Thy mercy, O Lord, is in the heavens, and thy faithfulness reacheth unto the clouds."

d) Lamentations 3:23—"Great is thy faithfulness."

e) Hebrews 10:23—"He is faithful that promised."

2. He preserves His people

God's faithfulness stands out especially in His preserving His people for glory. He secures our salvation.

a) 1 Thessalonians 5:23-24—"The very God of peace sanctify you wholly; and I pray God your whole spirit and soul and body be preserved blameless unto the coming of our Lord Jesus Christ. Faithful is he that calleth you, who also will do it."

b) Philippians 1:6—"[Be] confident of this very thing, that he who hath begun a good work in you will perform it until the day of Jesus Christ."

41

Review

The security of the believer is premised on the faithfulness of God. All the Scripture verses we have looked at, including Romans 5, describe God's implementation of His faithfulness. In Romans 5:1-11 Paul describes six links in an unbreakable chain that unites us to the Savior. So far we have examined three of them.

 I. PEACE WITH GOD (v. 1; see pp. 10-14)

"Being justified by faith, we have peace with God through our Lord Jesus Christ."

 II. STANDING IN GRACE (v. 2a; see pp. 15-20)

"By whom also we have access by faith into this grace in which we stand."

 III. HOPE OF GLORY (vv. 2b-5a; see pp. 28-37)

"[We] rejoice in hope of the glory of God. And not only so, but we glory in tribulations also, knowing that tribulation worketh patience; and patience, experience; and experience, hope; and hope maketh not ashamed."

Lesson

IV. POSSESSION OF LOVE (vv. 5b-8)

A. The Heart of Love (v. 5b)

"The love of God is shed abroad in our hearts by the Holy Spirit who is given unto us."

God has begun a love relationship with us that stretches throughout eternity.

1. The internal reality

a) Awareness

When you became a Christian, God deposited the Holy Spirit within you. In Ephesians 1:14 the apostle Paul calls the Holy Spirit the down payment—the guarantee of our salvation. We are guaranteed ultimate glory and ultimate salvation in heaven. The Holy Spirit then produces in us an awareness of God's love.

b) Assurance

The eighteenth-century hymn writer William Cowper wrote in "There Is a Fountain":

> E'er since by faith I saw the stream
> Thy flowing wounds supply,
> Redeeming love has been my theme
> And shall be till I die.

The most overwhelming concept in all Christianity is that God loves us. The personal, internal ministry of God through the Holy Spirit takes the issue of security beyond cognition to the deep recesses of the heart. By pouring out His love on us, God is assuring us in a subjective manner that we belong to Him.

(1) The presence of the Spirit

Romans 8:14 says, "For as many as are led by the Spirit of God, they are the sons of God." If you've ever been led to do anything for the glory of God—such as righteous behavior, faithful study of God's Word, prayer, or worship of the Lord Jesus Christ—the Holy Spirit has led you. If you have sensed the Holy Spirit's leading, you know you are a child of God. If you have ever felt led to cry out to God, "Abba, Father" (Rom. 8:15), you have sensed intimacy with God.

(2) The absence of the Spirit

The unregenerate individual senses no affinity, no intimacy, no communion with God. For those of us who know Jesus Christ, God has put His Spirit in us to draw us into an intimate love relationship with Himself.

Romans 5:5 says, "The love of God is shed abroad in our hearts." That doesn't refer to our love for God, but to God's love for us. Romans 5:8 says, "God commendeth His love toward us in that, while we were yet sinners, Christ died for us." God's love for us has been deposited in our hearts through the presence of the Holy Spirit. That means the Holy Spirit gives us the sense or feeling that God loves us.

c) Affection

We are emotional beings who respond to the Spirit of God. That truth solidifies everything we know intellectually about God. For example, we can know intellectually that we have peace with God because a divine transaction took place on the cross. We can know intellectually that we stand in grace and have been redeemed for future glory. But God goes beyond the intellectual, wanting us to feel His truth in our hearts. So His love is shed abroad in our hearts through the Holy Spirit.

Forfeiting Assurance

You can forfeit that subjective sense of assurance if you disobey God. Galatians 5:22 says, "The fruit of the Spirit is love, joy, [and] peace." Disobedience, unrighteousness, and unconfessed sin grieves or quenches the Spirit of God and hinders Him from bearing fruit through you. It is important to recognize that although God has put His love in our hearts through the Holy Spirit, we won't experience assurance unless we're walking in the Spirit.

Christians who disobey God do not have a sense of security in their salvation because they're leaning only on what is cognitive. They can say they have peace with God, stand in grace, and have hope of glory, but they don't experience the internal, subjective ministry of God's Spirit affirming that they belong to God. At that point

44

I know I'm saved because of the transaction at the cross that made peace and grace and hope a reality. But I also know I belong to Jesus Christ because the Holy Spirit reassures my spirit that I'm a child of God (Rom. 8:16).

2. The internal river

Romans 5:5 says that the love of God is "shed abroad" in our hearts. The Greek word translated "shed abroad" refers to something that is being poured out profusely or lavishly. God doesn't give us a little drop of love. John 7:38 says that when a man receives the Holy Spirit, "out of his heart shall flow rivers of living water." God never gives out anything in drops; He gives it out in rivers!

3. The internal revealer

a) The agency of the Spirit

According to Romans 5:5, God's love for us is made available through the Holy Spirit. He is the agent through whom God works in the life of the believer. He is the gift of God's love.

(1) The testimony of love

That the Holy Spirit lives within each believer is itself a great testimony to the love of God. Would God plant His Spirit—the third member of the Trinity—within you if He didn't love you?

(2) The guarantee of love

The Holy Spirit is the guarantee of our salvation, proving once and for all that our final salvation will come to pass (2 Cor. 1:22).

New International Version.

(3) The seal of love

Ephesians 1:13 says we are sealed by the Spirit—
sealed with the stamp of God—never to be bro-
ken or opened by anyone else.

b) The assurance of the Spirit

(1) We are conquerors through Christ

In Romans 8:35, 37-39 Paul says, "What shall separate us from the love of Christ? Shall tribulation,
or distress, or persecution, or famine, or naked-
ness, or peril, or sword? . . . Nay, in all these
things we are more than conquerors through him
that loved us. For I am persuaded that neither
death, nor life, nor angels, nor principalities, nor
powers, nor things present, nor things to come,
nor height, nor depth, nor any other creation,
shall be able to separate us from the love of God,
which is in Christ Jesus, our Lord." What can
separate us from the love of Christ? Nothing!

(2) We are confirmed through the Spirit

The sense of that assurance is confirmed by the
Holy Spirit Himself, God's blessed gift to us.
Based on Romans 5:5, no one can truly know the
love of God in his heart unless he has the Holy
Spirit living within him. Only those who have the
Holy Spirit in them are Christians. So if a Christian experiences a time when he loses the sense
of God's love for him, he undoubtedly has
quenched the ministry of the Holy Spirit.

B. The Height of Love (vv. 6-8)

"When we were yet without strength, in due time Christ
died for the ungodly. For scarcely for a righteous man will
one die; yet perhaps for a good man some would even dare
to die. But God commendeth his love toward us in that,
while we were yet sinners, Christ died for us."

1. The pitiful people (v. 6*a*)

"When we were yet without strength."

Prior to our salvation, we were powerless and totally unable to do anything that pleased God. We were without strength to overcome sin, Satan, the world, death, or hell. We couldn't live a righteous life or save ourselves because we were paralyzed by our sin. Romans 8:7 says we were at "enmity against God"—we were the enemies of holy God.

2. The compassionate Christ (v. 6*b*)

"In due time Christ died for the ungodly."

When God looked at us before we were saved, all that He saw in us filled Him with wrath and anger. Why? Because we were ungodly—the very opposite of Himself. It is amazing to realize that God, who is absolutely pure and holy, could still love beings who repulsed His holy nature. And He loved them so much that "in due time [at the time God prescribed] Christ died for the ungodly."

a) Sovereign love

(1) Constancy

It would be easy to understand God's loving those who are good, godly, and pure. But the mystery of divine love is that He loves those who are anything but that. Charles Hodge said, "If he loved us because we loved him, he would love us only so long as we love him, and on that condition; and then our salvation would depend on the constancy of our treacherous hearts. But as God loved us as sinners, as Christ died for us as ungodly, our salvation depends, as the apostle argues, not on our loveliness, but on the constancy of the love of God" (*Commentary on the Epistle to the Romans* [Grand Rapids: Eerdmans, 1974], pp. 136-37).

God doesn't love you because you're worthy of His love. Although human love is attracted by the nature of the object, God's love is built into His nature. There was nothing in us that attracted Him, yet He still loves us.

(2) Consistency

Since nothing in us caused God to love us in the first place, what could be in us to make Him stop loving us now? Nothing. Since Christ died for us when we were ungodly sinners, it isn't a problem for Him to love us now.

b) Substitutionary love

Romans 5:6 says that Christ died for the ungodly. The Greek word translated "for" (*huper*) is better translated "on behalf of," "instead of," or "for the sake of." Christ became a curse on our behalf (Gal. 3:13). At the proper moment in time, Christ put away sin through the sacrifice of Himself. The marvel of it all is that He lovingly died for such unlovely, godless people.

3. The supreme sacrifice (v. 7)

"Scarcely for a righteous man will one die, yet perhaps for a good man some would even dare to die."

The Greek words translated "righteous" and "good" are synonyms. There are times when someone might die for a good person. But the point of verse 7 is that no one would die for a bad person—no one, that is, except God.

4. The gracious God (v. 8)

"God commendeth his love toward us in that, while we were yet sinners, Christ died for us."

Our infinitely holy God is "of purer eyes than to behold evil, and canst not look on iniquity" (Hab. 1:13). The God who hates every sin—every evil deed, thought, and word—is the same God who reaches out and loves ungodly sinners. That is the surpassing nature of divine love. The Greek word translated "commendeth" means that God proved the nature of His love by having Christ die for us while we were yet sinners. That is the security of our salvation.

Since God loved us when we were ungodly, wicked sinners—since He loved us enough to let His Son die for us—will He not love us enough to keep us after we have become His children? When we were saved, we were wretched sinners. But we will never be again.

The love of God fills the heart of the believer. It's the kind of love that redeems a godless sinner. Since His love will do that, it will certainly hang onto a saint that sometimes still sins! And His forgiving love is poured into our hearts by the Holy Spirit. He loved us when we were wretched, and He still loves us now that we know Him.

V. CERTAINTY OF DELIVERANCE (vv. 9-10)

A. The Permanence of Our Salvation (v. 9)

"Much more then, being now justified by his blood, we shall be saved from wrath through him."

1. Its extent

In the past we were justified by Christ's blood, and in the future we will be saved from wrath through Him. By definition salvation is past, present, and future. We will be saved from wrath because biblically, there is no such thing as partial salvation. We were made right with God by the blood of Jesus Christ, and will be saved from the wrath to come through Him as well. The "wrath to come" is the lake of fire that burns with fire and brimstone, which is where the godless will be sent forever (Rev. 20:11-15).

2. Its essence

God is a God of wrath. But the wrath due to be poured out on all mankind was intercepted by Jesus. When we

49

put our faith in Him, God's wrath is set aside, and we are no longer children of wrath (Eph. 2:3). We have been saved from wrath. Paul reiterated that promise to the Thessalonians: "[We] wait for his Son from heaven, whom he raised from the dead, even Jesus, who delivered us from the wrath to come" (1 Thess. 1:10). No Christian will ever know the wrath of God. The full fury of God's wrath for your sin was poured out on Jesus Christ.

B. The Preservation of Our Salvation (v. 10)

"If, when we were enemies, we were reconciled to God by the death of his Son, much more, being reconciled, we shall be saved by his life."

1. Friendship with God

Since God brought us to Himself when we were enemies, we will be reconciled continually now that we are His friends. Sin can't prevent that from happening. When God first reconciled us, we were wretched, rotten, vile, godless sinners. Since that was not a barrier to His reconciliation then, there is nothing to keep Him from reconciling us now. Since He redeemed us when we were His enemies, He certainly will keep us now that we're His friends (John 15:15).

2. Fortification through Christ

Verse 10 says, "If, when we were enemies, we were reconciled to God by the death of his Son, much more, being reconciled, we shall be saved by his life." Through His death Jesus provided our salvation. So just imagine what He can do for us in His glorified resurrection life! Since God has done the greater act—saving us when we were wretched sinners—will He not do the lesser, which is to keep us?

All Through Jesus Christ

All that God did for us was accomplished through Jesus Christ. For example, verse 1 says, "We have peace with God through our Lord

Jesus Christ." Verse 2 says, "By whom also we have access." Verse 6 says, "In due time Christ died for the ungodly." Verse 8 says, "Christ died for us." Verse 9 says we are "justified by His blood" and "saved from wrath through Him." Verse 10 says we are "reconciled to God by the death of his Son" and "shall be saved by his life." Verse 11 says, "We also joy in God through our Lord Jesus Christ."

God never loved us because we were lovable; He saved us while we were in the midst of our sin. And He did it for His own glory—to show what a glorious, gracious, merciful, and loving God He is (Eph. 1:5-6). What kind of God would He be if He turned His back on us now? He would receive no glory for that. But He reconciled us to Himself through Christ (2 Cor. 5:20-21).

Hebrews 7:25 says, "He is able also to save them to the uttermost that come unto God by him." When you come to God through Jesus Christ, He will save you to the uttermost—to the fullest point of salvation. How can He do that? Verse 25 continues: "Seeing he ever liveth to make intercession for them." Christ can save us by His life because He is alive right now at the right hand of the Father, interceding for us. He takes our case before the Father and pleads it on our behalf. He tells God that He bore our sin and received God's judgment and wrath. For that reason we are to be forgiven. He continually intercedes for us, and thus carries our salvation to its uttermost point, which is our glorification (Rom. 8:30). When Jesus said, "Because I live, ye shall live also" (John 14:19), He was referring to His continual intercession on our behalf.

VI. JOY IN GOD (v. 11)

"We also joy in God through our Lord Jesus Christ, by whom we have now received the reconciliation."

A. The Origin of Joy

Another subjective reality of our belonging to God is a heart filled with joy. Galatians 5:22 says, "The fruit of the Spirit is love [and] joy." Salvation is not merely a future

51

hope but a present and abundant joy. Internal joy is one of the great securities of salvation. This is the third time Paul has referred to our rejoicing in God (cf. Rom. 5:2-3). The Greek word translated "joy" means "to exult," "to rejoice jubilantly," or "to be thrilled." So our present sense of internal joy is an additional guarantee of our future salvation.

B. The Object of Joy

The focus of the believer's joy is God Himself—not the believer's own righteousness, ability, or worthiness. That's why the psalmist said, "Oh, magnify the Lord with me, and let us exalt his name together" (Ps. 34:3). In the midst of death or disaster, we don't lose our perspective because we rejoice in a God who keeps His own. The psalmist also said, "My soul shall be joyful in the Lord; it shall rejoice in his salvation" (Ps. 35:9). Psalm 43:4 says, "Then will I go unto the altar of God, unto God, my exceeding joy." We don't boast or rejoice in ourselves—we rejoice in God.

The final link that anchors us to our blessed Savior, the Lord Jesus Christ, is our joy in God. It is through Christ that we have received reconciliation with God. And that makes us secure!

Focusing on the Facts

1. What attribute of God is the foundation of everything the Christian believes in (see p. 41)?
2. In what way does God's faithfulness especially stand out (see p. 41)?
3. Why did Paul refer to the Holy Spirit as the guarantee of our salvation (see p. 43)?
4. Why does God give us a subjective assurance of salvation (see p. 43)?
5. How does the believer know that God loves him (see p. 44)?
6. How can a believer forfeit the sense of his assurance? Explain (see pp. 44-45).
7. Why do we need an internal, subjective assurance of salvation in addition to a cognitive assurance (see pp. 44-45)?
8. How much does God love the believer (see p. 45)?

9. Why were we without strength to please God (see p. 47)?
10. What is the mystery of God's love? Why is it a mystery (see pp. 47-48)?
11. Why is God's present love for us so secure (see p. 48)?
12. How did God prove His love for us (Rom. 5:8; see pp. 48-49)?
13. What does the believer's salvation encompass (see p. 49)?
14. How do we know that God keeps us in a constant state of reconciliation (see p. 50)?
15. Why did God save us (see p. 51)?

Pondering the Principles

1. Are you a faithful person? Do you tend to do the things you say you are going to do? Contrast God's faithfulness with your own. List as many reasons as you can for trusting God's faithfulness. Based on your response, how can you best encourage people who are enduring trials?

2. Memorize Romans 5:8: "God demonstrates His own love toward us, in that while we were yet sinners, Christ died for us" (NASB*). Replace the words *us* and *we* with your name. What does that verse mean to you? Meditate on your answer, and thank God for His love.

3. Look up the following verses: John 5:26; 10:28-29; 14:19; Romans 8:34-39; Colossians 3:3-4; Revelation 1:18. List all the securities you can find. How does Christ save you by His life? What are the chances of your losing your salvation? As a result of knowing how secure you are, what kind of changes do you need to make in your life to bring God the most glory? Prayerfully consider the steps you need to make to implement those changes.

New American Standard Bible.

4
The Doctrine of Salvation—Assurance

Outline

Lesson
I. Two Questions on Assurance
  A. Is Salvation Secure?
    1. The sovereign decree of the Father
      a) John 5:24
      b) John 3:16, 18
      c) John 6:37-40
    2. The high-priestly work of Jesus Christ
      a) John 17:11, 15
      b) John 10:27-29
    3. The affirmation of Scripture
      a) 1 Peter 1:3-5
      b) 1 John 2:1-2
  B. Can We Experience That Security?
    1. Pure doctrine
      a) 2 John 9
      b) Colossians 1:22-23
    2. Pure living
      a) Righteousness
        (1) Bearing fruit
        (2) Denying ungodliness
      b) Remembrance
        (1) The reality of our salvation (2 Pet. 1:1-2)
          (*a*) The equality of faith
          (*b*) The establishment of faith
          (*c*) The enlightenment of faith
        (2) The riches of our salvation (2 Pet. 1:3-4)
          (*a*) The gifts
          (*b*) The glory
          (*c*) The grant

Lesson

I. TWO QUESTIONS ON ASSURANCE

Can we be assured of our salvation? To answer that we need to answer two other questions: Is our salvation secure? and, Can we experience that security? We can't answer the second without answering the first.

A. Is Salvation Secure?

The answer is yes. But we need to support that answer biblically. I believe Scripture makes it abundantly clear that our salvation is secure.

1. The sovereign decree of the Father

a) John 5:24—Jesus said, "He that heareth my word, and believeth on him that sent me, hath everlasting life, and shall not come into judgment, but is passed from death unto life." That may be the most monumental statement ever made in the Bible relative to the security of salvation. The believer has received everlasting life and will not come under judgment.

b) John 3:16, 18—"God so loved the world, that he gave his only begotten Son, that whosoever believeth in him should not perish, but have everlasting life. . . . He that believeth on him is not condemned; but he that believeth not is condemned already." On the positive side, the verses tell us that we have everlasting life; on the negative side, they tell us that we will never come into judgment.

c) John 6:37-40—Jesus said, "All that the Father giveth me shall come to me" (v. 37). All whom God sovereignly chooses will come to Christ. However, that should not restrain any one from coming to Christ, for He said, "Him that cometh to me I will in no wise cast out" (v. 37).

In verses 38-39 Jesus says, "I came down from heaven, not to do mine own will but the will of him that sent me. And this is the Father's will who hath sent me, that of all that he hath given me I should lose nothing, but should raise it up again at the last day." All those chosen for salvation—all those who came to Jesus Christ—will be raised up on the last day. Not one will be lost.

In verse 40 Jesus sums up His teaching: "This is the will of him that sent me, that everyone who seeth the Son, and believeth on him, may have everlasting life; and I will raise him up at the last day." Whoever believes in Christ will be raised up to the fullness of eternal life. That is the promise of God's Word.

2. The high-priestly work of Jesus Christ

a) John 17:11, 15—Jesus prayed for His disciples in anticipation of His departure from the world, saying, "Now I am no more in the world, but these are in the world, and I come to thee. Holy Father, keep through thine own name those whom thou hast given me. . . . I pray not that thou shouldest take them out of the world, but that thou shouldest keep them from the evil [one]." Since our Savior always prays in perfect harmony with the will of the Father, we can be assured that this is the will of God.

b) John 10:27-29—Jesus said, "My sheep hear my voice, and I know them, and they follow me" (v. 27). The true sheep are committed to the true shepherd. In verses 28-29 Jesus says, "I give unto them eternal life;

and they shall never perish, neither shall any man pluck them out of my hand. My Father, who gave them to me, is greater than all, and no man is able to pluck them out of my Father's hand." On the positive side, Jesus assures us that we have everlasting life; on the negative side, He assures us that no one will ever be removed out of his eternal relationship with the Father.

We are secured by the sovereign purpose of God and the continual, faithful intercession of our great High Priest—the Lord Jesus Christ. Jude 24 says, "Unto him that is able to keep you from falling, and to present you faultless before the presence of his glory with exceeding joy." We know from the high-priestly prayer of the Lord Jesus Christ that He is able to keep us from falling.

3. The affirmation of Scripture

   a) 1 Peter 1:3-5—"[God] hath begotten us again unto a living hope by the resurrection of Jesus Christ from the dead, to an inheritance incorruptible, and undefiled, and that fadeth not away, reserved in heaven for you, who are kept by the power of God through faith unto salvation ready to be revealed in the last time." Our inheritance is permanent. Those God saves He glorifies (cf. Rom. 8:30).

   b) 1 John 2:1-2—Does God's promise still hold true when we sin? The apostle John said, "If any man sin, we have an advocate with the Father, Jesus Christ the righteous; and he is the propitiation [satisfaction] for our sins." If any man sins we have a lawyer for the defense, Jesus Christ, who goes to the Father and tells Him not to hold any sin against a believer, for He, Christ, has paid sin's penalty in full.

B. Can We Experience That Security?

Can we know that we are secure? Yes. How do we know? Many claim that they remember the day they signed a card, walked the aisle, raised their hand, or were baptized. But none of those things are valid proofs for affirming your salvation, nor is regular church attendance.

Why Do So Many Doubt Their Salvation?

Many people do not enjoy the assurance of their salvation. "Assurance" is a more accurate word to use in this section than "security." That is because security refers to the facts, whereas assurance refers to the feeling of knowing you are secure. Assurance, just like any other blessing of God, can be forfeited through disobedience. Whenever a person is not sure if he is saved, there are several possibilities. First, he may not be saved. Second, he may be disobeying God. And third, he may be being buffeted by Satan, the liar of all liars, who wants us to doubt what in fact is true. Against Satan's attack the believer must affirm what Paul says in Romans 8:31-39—that no one can lay any charge to God's elect because God has justified them.

The New Testament teaches us two ways we can experience assurance.

1. Pure doctrine

One of the internal evidences—one of the things that gives us a sense of knowing we're saved—is our abiding in doctrine that is correct.

a) 2 John 9—"Whosoever trangresseth, and abideth not in the doctrine of Christ, hath not God. He that abideth in the doctrine of Christ, he hath both the Father and the Son." True assurance is available only to those who abide in the true biblical doctrine of Christ. If you have a wrong view of Jesus Christ, you will not experience security in your salvation. People who follow the teachings of cults or unbiblical religions, and do not affirm the Christ of the Bible, will never experience a genuine sense of assurance. That's why they work so frantically to earn salvation. They try to be affirmed by their works because they never experience assurance.

b) Colossians 1:22-23—"In the body of his flesh through death, to present you holy and unblamable and unreprovable in his sight, if ye continue in the faith grounded and settled, and be not moved away from the hope of the gospel." Internal assurance comes when there is no deviation in doctrine—when we affirm the Christ of the gospel and the gospel of Christ.

2. Pure living

Pure living is the key to experiencing assurance in your salvation.

a) Righteousness

If you look at your life and see nothing but compromise and corruption, don't be surprised if you don't have any sense of security.

(1) Bearing fruit

In Matthew 7:18 Jesus gives the following truism: "A good tree cannot bring forth bad fruit, neither can a corrupt tree bring forth good fruit." If you see corrupt fruit in your life, it's logical to assume you're a corrupt tree. It is vital that you see a pattern of holy living in your life if you are ever to know assurance. If you don't see that pattern, there is no way you can logically conclude that you're saved.

(2) Denying ungodliness

In Titus 2:11-14 Paul says, "The grace of God that bringeth salvation hath appeared to all men, teaching us that, denying ungodliness and worldly lusts, we should live soberly, righteously, and godly, in this present age, looking for that blessed hope, and the glorious appearing of the great God and our Savior, Jesus Christ, who gave himself for us that he might redeem us from all iniquity, and purify unto himself a people of his own, zealous of good works." Salvation teaches you to deny ungodliness. Therefore, if you are not denying ungodliness in your life, you will have a difficult time believing you are really saved. James says that faith without works is dead (James 2:17).

b) Remembrance

In 2 Peter 1:12 Peter says, "I will not be negligent to put you always in remembrance of these things, though ye know them, and are established in the present truth." "These things" refer to what Peter said in the first eleven verses. He wanted the believers to remember and be established in the things they already knew about their salvation.

(1) The reality of our salvation (2 Pet. 1:1-2)

Second Peter begins: "Simon Peter, a servant and apostle of Jesus Christ, to them that have obtained like precious faith with us through the righteousness of God and our Savior, Jesus Christ: grace and peace be multiplied unto you through the knowledge of God, and of Jesus, our Lord" (vv. 1-2).

(a) The equality of faith

Peter said we have "obtained" salvation. It is a gift, not something we purchased. The phrase "like precious faith" refers to saving faith or the act of believing. That faith is considered precious—it is highly valuable. Also, it is "like" the faith of other believers. Everyone comes to Christ on the same terms: faith. Our Savior saves us all equally. There is no distinction (Matt. 19:30–20:16).

(b) The establishment of faith

Salvation is a result of "the righteousness of God and our Savior, Jesus Christ." God has granted us His righteousness and holiness, which is the essence of His nature.

(c) The enlightenment of faith

God granted us His righteousness and holiness "through the knowledge [Gk., *epignosis*, "deep, profound knowledge"] of God, and Jesus, our Lord." When a person acquires deep knowledge of God, he receives the righteousness of God and Christ.

(2) The riches of our salvation (2 Pet. 1:3-4)

(a) The gifts

Verse 3 says, "According as his divine power hath given unto us all things that pertain unto life and godliness." The phrase "divine power" means that God, with His infinite energy, dispensed His eternal resources to us.

(b) The glory

Those resources came to us "through the knowledge of him that called us to glory and virtue" (v. 3). God called us to glory (the essence of the life of God in the soul of man) and to virtue (the manifestation of the life of God in the soul of man). We have been given everything we need and have been called to manifest the life of God within us.

(c) The grant

In verse 4 Peter says, "By which are given unto us exceedingly great and precious [priceless] promises, that by these ye might be partakers of the divine nature." The apostle Paul said, "I am crucified with Christ; nevertheless I live; yet not I, but Christ liveth in me" (Gal. 2:20). He also said, "Christ in you [is] the hope of glory" (Col. 1:27). As a result of receiving precious promises and becoming partakers of the divine nature, we have "escaped the corruption that is in the world through lust" (2 Pet. 1:4).

(3) The responsibility inherent in our salvation (2 Pet. 1:5-7)

Verse 5 says, "Beside this, giving all diligence." There's a responsibility inherent in our salvation. Those who advocate the doctrine of total surrender—of merely letting go and letting God—have trouble reconciling this verse. Peter continues, "Giving all diligence, add to your faith." Peter was not saying we're to do that apart from the Holy Spirit. We're to add to our faith the following:

(a) Virtue

The Greek word translated "virtue" (aretē) refers to the excellence of a thing. What is the excellence of any man or woman? "The measure of the stature of the fullness of Christ" (Eph. 4:13).

(b) Knowledge

To our excellence we are to add "knowledge" (Gk., gnōsis), which refers to practical wisdom.

(c) Self-control

To our knowledge we are to add "self-control." That means we need to discipline ourselves not to fall into our old habits of sin.

(d) Patience

To self-control we're to add "patience" (Gk., hupomonē). That means we're to persevere in what is right no matter the cost.

(e) Godliness

To patience we're to add "godliness" (Gk., eusebeia), which is reverence and awe of God.

(f) Brotherly kindness

To godliness we're to add "brotherly kindness" (Gk., *philadelphia*).

(g) Love

To brotherly kindness we're to add love, which is unselfish service rendered on behalf of others.

(4) The result of our salvation (2 Pet. 1:8)

In verse 8 Peter says, "If these things [virtue, knowledge, self-control, patience, godliness, brotherly kindness, and love] be in you and abound . . ." That means those things should be increasing in a believer's life. We will not attain perfection until we see Christ, but that should be the direction we're moving in.

If those things Peter mentioned in verses 5-7 characterize your life, "they make you that ye shall neither be barren nor unfruitful in the knowledge of our Lord Jesus Christ" (v. 8). I can't think of anything worse than a barren and unfruitful Christian. Verse 8 implies that you can possess the divine nature and the exceeding precious promises of God, have escaped the corruption of the world, know God through Jesus Christ, have the righteousness of Christ imputed to you, and have all things pertaining to life and godliness, yet experience times of barrenness and unfruitfulness in your life. Why? Simply by not adding the things of verses 5-7 to the substance of your faith in the power of the Spirit.

The point of verse 8 is clear: When those characteristics are not increasing in your life, you become indistinguishable from an apostate. Therefore, you will have no sense of assurance because you won't be able to see any difference between yourself and an unbeliever.

(5) The rest of our salvation (2 Pet. 1:9-11)

    (*a*) The loss of eternal perspective

        i) Blindness

In verse 9 Peter says, "He that lacketh these things is blind and cannot see afar off." The Greek word translated "afar off" is the basis for the English word *myopic*, which means, "to be nearsighted." A person with myopia has lost his ability to see into the distance. Peter's point is that the believer has lost his eternal perspective. All he sees is what is immediately before him. Spiritual myopia focuses on the passing things of the earth. Paul refers to man's blindness in a different context in 2 Corinthians 4:4: "The god of this age hath blinded the minds of them who believe not." Unbelievers are totally blind, and a believer appears no different when his focus is on the world.

If you can't see the things of verses 5-7 in your life, you have lost your eternal perspective. If you aren't being fruitful, you have become trapped in the world's environment.

        ii) Forgetfulness

The believer with spiritual myopia "hath forgotten that he was purged from his old sins" (v. 9). The Greek word translated "purged" (*katharismos*) refers to a cleansing from the sins of the past. So Peter is saying that a person who has spiritual myopia will have forgotten that he was saved.

Assurance in a believer's life is directly related to an increase in the spiritual graces outlined in verses 5-7.

(*b*) The life of eternal reward

In verse 10 Peter says, "Wherefore the rather, brethren, give diligence to make your calling and election sure; for if ye do these things, ye shall never fall." Believers don't want to live without the assurance of their salvation, so it's imperative for them to make sure of their calling and election. Then they won't fall from their sense of security.

The Greek text of verse 11 is best translated: "For so richly will be supplied to you entrance into the eternal Kingdom of our Lord and Savior Jesus Christ." If you add the things of verses 5-7 to your life, you will make your calling and election sure, you will not fall from your confidence, and you will receive all that is coming to you (when you meet Jesus Christ).

II. TWELVE TESTS ON ASSURANCE

A. Do You Enjoy Fellowship with Christ and His Redeemed People?

If you regularly participate in such fellowship, that's a sign you are a Christian (cf. Heb. 10:24-26). First John 1:3 says, "That which we have seen and heard declare we unto you, that ye also may have fellowship with us; and truly our fellowship is with the Father, and with His Son, Jesus Christ." We have fellowship with God the Father, God the Son, and everyone who has fellowship with the Father and the Son. When you were saved you entered into fellowship with Jesus Christ and His redeemed people. If you have shared in the prayers, praises, and testimonies of God's people, that's an indication you belong to Him.

B. Are You Sensitive to Your Sin?

First John 1:8, 10 says "If we say that we have no sin, we deceive ourselves, and the truth is not in us. . . . If we say that we have not sinned, we make him a liar, and his word is not in us." If you have a continual sensitivity to the sin in your life and are in awe of holy God, that's an indication you are a Christian.

C. Do You Tend to Hate the World and Its Evil?

First John 2:15 says, "Love not the world, neither the things that are in the world. If any man love the world, the love of the Father is not in him." If you love the system of the world and all that it stands for, that indicates you are not a Christian. However, if you have a basic hatred of the evil in this world, even though you may fall into its trap now and then, that's an indication you are a Christian.

D. Are You Obedient to God's Word?

First John 2:3-5 says, "By this we do know that we know him, if we keep his commandments. He that saith, I know him, and keepeth not his commandments, is a liar, and the truth is not in him. But whosoever keepeth his word, in him verily is the love of God perfected; by this know we that we are in him."

E. Do You Await the Coming of Jesus Christ?

First John 3:2-3 says, "Beloved . . . it doth not yet appear what we shall be, but we know that, when he shall appear, we shall be like him; for we shall see him as he is. And every man that hath this hope in him purifieth himself even as he is pure." If you love Christ and eagerly await His coming, that indicates you are a Christian.

F. Do You See a Decreasing Pattern of Sin in Your Life?

First John 3:5-6 says, "Ye know that he was manifest to take away our sins, and in him is no sin. Whosoever abideth in him sinneth not; whosoever sinneth hath not seen him, neither known him." A true Christian will experience a decreasing frequency of sin in his life.

G. Do You Make Sacrifices for Other Christians?

First John 3:14 says, "We know that we have passed from death unto life, because we love the brethren. He that loveth not his brother abideth in death." Then in verses 16-17

John says, "We ought to lay down our lives for the brethren. But whosoever hath this world's good, and seeth his brother have need, and shutteth up his compassions from him, how dwelleth the love of God in him?"

H. Do You Experience Answered Prayer?

First John 3:22 says, "Whatever we ask, we receive of him, because we keep his commandments, and do those things that are pleasing in his sight." Answered prayer is the result of keeping God's commandments and doing what is pleasing in His sight. So if you're seeing answers to your prayers, that indicates you are a Christian.

I. Do You Experience the Internal Work of the Holy Spirit?

First John 3:24 says, "By this we know that he abideth in us, by the Spirit whom he hath given us." John also says, "By this know we that we dwell in him, and he in us, because he hath given us of his Spirit" (1 John 4:13). The Spirit in us cries, "Abba, Father" (Rom. 8:15; Gal. 4:6). Although you may be experiencing doubt at the present time, if you can look back and see the Spirit's leading in the past, that's an affirmation that you belong to God.

J. Are You Able to Discern Between Spiritual Truth and Error?

First John 4:1-6 says, "Believe not every spirit, but test the spirits whether they are of God; because many false prophets are gone out into the world. By this know ye the Spirit of God: every spirit that confesseth that Jesus Christ is come in the flesh is of God; and every spirit that confesseth not that Jesus Christ is come in the flesh is not of God; and this is that spirit of antichrist, of which ye have heard that it should come, and even now already is in the world. Ye are of God, little children, and have overcome them, because greater is he that is in you, than he that is in the world. They are of the world; therefore speak they of the world, and the world heareth them. We are of God. He that knoweth God heareth us; he that is not of God heareth not us. By this know we the spirit of truth, and the spirit of error." A true Christian does not fall prey to false teaching about Jesus Christ, the doctrine of salvation, and other basics of the faith.

K. Do You Believe What the Bible Teaches?

First John 5:1 says, "Whosoever believeth that Jesus is the Christ is born of God." Why should you believe that? Because the Bible, which proves itself to be the Word of God, says so.

L. Have You Ever Suffered on Account of Your Faith?

The devil doesn't attack the tares; he attacks the wheat (Matt. 13:24-30, 36-43). Philippians 1:28 says, "In nothing [be] terrified by your adversaries, which is to them an evident token of perdition, but to you of salvation." When you are attacked by the enemy, remember that he is judged, but you are saved.

Focusing on the Facts

1. How does the Bible affirm the security of our salvation (see pp. 56-58)?
2. What does Jesus say about everlasting life (John 3:16, 18; 5:24; see pp. 56-57)?
3. According to John 6:37-40, what happens to those who have been chosen for salvation (see p. 57)?
4. What does Jesus Christ do when we sin? Why is He able to do that (see p. 58)?
5. What are three reasons some people don't have an assurance of their salvation (see p. 59)?
6. What are the two basic ways that the New Testament teaches us how to experience the assurance of our salvation (see pp. 59-60)?
7. Why do those who do not affirm the Christ of the Bible never experience a genuine sense of assurance (see p. 59)?
8. Why is it important for a believer to see a pattern of holy living in his life (see p. 60)?
9. What does "like precious faith" mean (2 Pet. 1:1; see p. 61)?
10. What are the riches of our salvation (see p. 62)?
11. To what have Christians been called (2 Pet. 1:3; see p. 62)?

12. What are we to add to our saving faith? Explain each (see pp. 63-64).
13. What should be the direction of your life (see p. 64)?
14. How can you possess the realities and the riches of salvation yet still experience times of barrenness and unfruitfulness (see p. 64)?
15. What happens when you don't add to your faith the things mentioned in 2 Peter 1:5-7 (see p. 65)?
16. What happens when you add to your faith the characteristics mentioned in 2 Peter 1:5-7 (see p. 66)?
17. Why is fellowship with Christ and His people an indication of salvation (1 John 1:3; see p. 66)?
18. Why is sensitivity to sin an indication of salvation (1 John 1:8, 10; see pp. 66-67)?
19. Why is answered prayer a proof of salvation (1 John 3:22; see p. 68)?
20. Why doesn't a true Christian fall prey to false teaching (1 John 4:1-6; see pp. 68-69)?
21. Why is an attack on our faith an indication of our salvation (Phil. 1:28; see p. 69)?

Pondering the Principles

1. Read Romans 8:28-39. In a short paragraph, explain the security you have as a Christian. What verses indicate the sovereign decree of God in your salvation? What verses indicate the high-priestly work of Christ? Find other Scripture verses that affirm Romans 8:28-39. Which ones stand out to you? Choose one to memorize.

2. List the twelve tests of assurance (see pp. 66-69). On a scale of one to ten, rate yourself in regard to how each test affirms your security. Why do you have a low rating in some areas and a high rating in others? Read 1 John 3:19-21. Does your heart condemn you in some of those areas? Then read Romans 8:1. Who is greater than your heart? If Jesus Christ is your Savior and Lord, you are no longer condemned. Is He your Savior and Lord? Prayerfully consider 2 Corinthians 13:5.

Scripture Index

Topical Index